■SCHOLASTIC

READ&RES____

Bringing the best books to life in the classroom

Activities based on **One Dog and His Boy**
By Eva Ibbotson

Recommended system requirements:
Windows: XP (Service Pack 3), Vista (Service Pack 2), Windows 7 or Windows 8 with 2.33GHz processor
Mac: OS 10.6 to 10.8 with Intel Core™ Duo processor
1GB RAM (recommended)
1024 x 768 Screen resolution
CD-ROM drive (24x speed recommended)
Adobe Reader (version 9 recommended for Mac users)
Broadband internet connections (for installation and updates)

For all technical support queries (including no CD drive), please phone Scholastic Customer Services on 0845 6039091.

Designed using Adobe Indesign

Scholastic Education, an imprint of Scholastic Ltd

Book End, Range Road, Witney, Oxfordshire, OX29 0YD

Registered office: Westfield Road, Southam,

Warwickshire CV47 0RA

www.scholastic.co.uk

Printed and bound by Ashford Colour Press

© 2016 Scholastic Ltd

1 2 3 4 5 6 7 8 9   6 7 8 9 0 1 2 3 4 5

British Library Cataloguing-in-Publication Data

A catalogue record for this book is available from the British Library.

ISBN 978-1407-14230-2

Author Jillian Powell

Editorial team Rachel Morgan, Jenny Wilcox, Suzanne Adams, Elizabeth Evans

Series designer Neil Salt

Designer Anna Oliwa

Illustrator Mike Lacey/Beehive Illustration

Digital development Hannah Barnett, Phil Crothers and MWA Technologies Private Ltd

Acknowledgements

The publishers gratefully acknowledge permission to reproduce the following copyright material:

Scholastic Children's Books for permission to use the cover and the text from *One Dog and His Boy* by Eva Ibbotson. Text © Eva Ibbotson, 2011. Illustration © Sharon Rentta, 2011. Reproduced with the permission of Scholastic Ltd. All Rights Reserved.

Every effort has been made to trace copyright holders for the works reproduced in this book, and the publishers apologise for any inadvertent omissions.

CONTENTS

INTRODUCTION

Read & Respond provides teaching ideas related to a specific children's book. The series focuses on best-loved books and brings you ways to use them to engage your class and enthuse them about reading.

The book is divided into different sections:

- **About the book and author:** gives you some background information about the book and the author.

- **Guided reading:** breaks the book down into sections and gives notes for using it with guided reading groups. A bookmark has been provided on page 12 containing comprehension questions. The children can be directed to refer to these as they read.

- **Shared reading:** provides extracts from the children's books with associated notes for focused work. There is also one non-fiction extract that relates to the children's book.

- **Grammar, punctuation & spelling:** provides word-level work related to the children's book so you can teach grammar, punctuation and spelling in context.

- **Plot, character & setting:** contains activity ideas focused on the plot, characters and the setting of the story.

- **Talk about it:** has speaking and listening activities related to the children's book. These activities may be based directly on the children's book or be broadly based on the themes and concepts of the story.

- **Get writing:** provides writing activities related to the children's book. These activities may be based directly on the children's book or be broadly based on the themes and concepts of the story.

- **Assessment:** contains short activities that will help you assess whether the children have understood concepts and curriculum objectives. They are designed to be informal activities to feed into your planning.

The activities follow the same format:

- **Objective:** the objective for the lesson. It will be based upon a curriculum objective, but will often be more specific to the focus being covered.

- **What you need:** a list of resources you need to teach the lesson, including digital resources (printable pages, interactive activities and media resources, see page 5).

- **What to do:** the activity notes.

- **Differentiation:** this is provided where specific and useful differentiation advice can be given to support and/or extend the learning in the activity. Differentiation by providing additional adult support has not been included as this will be at a teacher's discretion based upon specific children's needs and ability, as well as the availability of support.

The activities are numbered for reference within each section and should move through the text sequentially – so you can use the lesson while you are reading the book. Once you have read the book, most of the activities can be used in any order you wish.

Below are brief guidance notes for using the CD-ROM. For more detailed information, please click on the '?' button in the top right-hand corner of the screen.

The program contains the following:
* the extract pages from the book
* all of the photocopiable pages from the book
* additional printable pages
* interactive on-screen activities
* media resources.

Getting started

Put the CD-ROM into your CD-ROM drive. If you do not have a CD-ROM drive, phone Scholastic Customer Services on 0845 6039091.

* For Windows users, the install wizard should autorun. If it fails to do so, then navigate to your CD-ROM drive and follow the installation process.
* For Mac users, copy the disk image file to your hard drive. After it has finished copying, double click it to mount the disk image. Navigate to the mounted disk image and run the installer. After installation, the disk image can be unmounted and the DMG can be deleted from the hard drive.
* To install on a network, see the ReadMe file located on the CD-ROM (navigate to your drive).

To complete the installation of the program you need to open the program and click 'Update' in the pop-up. Please note – this CD-ROM is web-enabled and the content will be downloaded from the internet to your hard drive to populate the CD-ROM with the relevant resources. This only needs to be done on first use, after this you will be able to use the CD-ROM without an internet connection. If at any point any content is updated, you will receive another pop-up upon start up when there is an internet connection.

Main menu

The main menu is the first screen that appears. Here you can access: terms and conditions, registration links, how to use the CD-ROM and credits. To access a specific book click on the relevant button (only titles installed will be available). You can filter by the

drop-down lists if you wish. You can search all resources by clicking 'Search' in the bottom left-hand corner. You can also log in and access favourites that you have bookmarked.

Resources

By clicking on a book on the Main menu, you are taken to the resources for that title. The resources are: Media, Interactives, Extracts and Printables. Select the category and then launch a resource by clicking the play button.

Teacher settings

In the top right-hand corner of the screen is a small 'T' icon. This is the teacher settings area. It is password protected, the password is: login. This area will allow you to choose the print quality settings for interactive activities ('Default' or 'Best') and also allow you to check for updates to the program or re-download all content to the disk via 'Refresh all content'. You can also set up user logins so that you can save and access favourites. Once a user is set up, they can enter by clicking the login link underneath the 'T' and '?' buttons.

Search

You can access an all resources search by clicking the search button on the bottom left of the Main menu. You can search for activities by type (using the drop-down filter) or by keyword by typing into the box. You can then assign resources to your favourites area or launch them directly from the search area.

CURRICULUM LINKS

Section	Activity	Curriculum objectives
Guided reading		Comprehension: To explain and discuss their understanding of what they have read and provide reasoned justifications for their views; to identify and discuss themes.
Shared reading	1	Comprehension: To explain and discuss their understanding of what they have read and provide reasoned justifications for their views; to draw inferences such as inferring characters' feelings, justifying inferences with evidence.
	2	Comprehension: To discuss and evaluate the author's use of figurative language.
	3	Comprehension: To draw inferences, justifying inferences with evidence; to discuss and evaluate the author's use of figurative language.
	4	Comprehension: To retrieve and present information from non-fiction.
Grammar, punctuation & spelling	1	Composition: To use relative clauses; to use commas to clarify meaning.
	2	Composition: To find and use synonyms and antonyms.
	3	Composition: To understand and use the passive voice.
	4	Composition: To use adverbials.
	5	Composition: To use a colon to introduce a list and to use semicolons and bullet points within lists.
	6	Transcription: To investigate spellings and learn some words specifically.
Plot, character & setting	1	Comprehension: To draw inferences, justifying them with evidence.
	2	Composition: To describe characters.
	3	Comprehension: To draw inferences, justifying them with evidence; to ask questions to improve understanding.
	4	Comprehension: To identify how language and structure contribute to meaning.
	5	Composition: To describe settings.
	6	Comprehension: To summarise the main ideas drawn from more than one paragraph.
	7	Comprehension: To summarise the main ideas drawn from more than one paragraph; to explain their understanding of what they have read, including through presentations.
	8	Comprehension: To identify how structure contributes to meaning; to discuss how authors use language, considering the impact on the reader.

Section	Activity	Curriculum objectives
Talk about it	1	Spoken language: To use spoken language to develop understanding through speculating, hypothesising, imagining and exploring ideas. Comprehension: To précis longer passages.
	2	Spoken language: To articulate and justify opinions; to participate in discussions. Comprehension: To explain and discuss their understanding of what they have read.
	3	Spoken language: To participate in discussions, presentations and role play. Comprehension: To draw inferences, such as inferring characters' feelings, thoughts and motives.
	4	Spoken language: To articulate and justify opinions; to participate in discussions and debates.
	5	Comprehension: To explain and discuss their understanding of what they have read; to provide reasoned justifications for their views. Spoken language: To participate in debates.
	6	Comprehension: To explain and discuss their understanding of what they have read; to provide reasoned justifications for their views.
Get writing	1	Composition: To describe settings, characters and atmosphere.
	2	Composition: To identify audience and select appropriate form for purpose of writing.
	3	Spoken language: To participate in role play and improvisations. Composition: To perform their own compositions.
	4	Comprehension: To retrieve, record and present information from non-fiction. Composition: To plan their writing by selecting the appropriate form.
	5	Comprehension: To draw inferences, such as inferring characters' thoughts, feelings and motives. Composition: To select appropriate form for purpose of writing.
	6	Composition: To plan their writing by noting and developing initial ideas; to describe characters in narratives.
Assessment	1	Composition: To describe characters. Spoken language: To maintain attention, staying on topic and initiating and responding to comments.
	2	Comprehension: To identify and discuss themes. Spoken language: To participate in discussions and presentations.
	3	Transcription: To investigate spelling and understand that the meaning of some words needs to be learned specifically.
	4	Comprehension: To ask questions to improve understanding; to identify and discuss themes and conventions.
	5	Spoken language: To give well-structured explanations, including expressing feelings; to articulate and justify answers, arguments and opinions.
	6	Spoken language: To articulate and justify answers, arguments and opinions; to participate in discussions and presentations.

ONE DOG AND HIS BOY

About the book

One Dog and His Boy was Eva Ibbotson's penultimate book, written in the animal adventure genre of Dodie Smith's *The Hundred and One Dalmatians* and Michael Morpurgo's *Shadow*. Its themes of friendship, loyalty and following one's dreams are underpinned with a strong moral: that material things are worthless in comparison with love, loyalty and companionship. Hal is a boy who has everything except what he most wants in the world: a canine companion. His parents have become so embroiled in their superficial world of financial and material success that they neglect Hal's emotional needs and well-being, thinking that if they rent a dog from the Easy Pets Dog Agency, he will soon tire of it as quickly as he does his expensive toys. But they have underestimated the bond that Hal instantly forms with the little mongrel that comes to stay for the weekend. When Hal finally finds his heart's desire in Fleck, only to lose him when he is returned to the Agency, the two must go on a long adventure, battling the odds to be together and achieve their happy ending.

About the author

Eva Ibbotson was born in Vienna in 1925, into a Jewish family living in Austria. Her parents separated when she was two, and her father, who was a physician, moved to Scotland to take up a job in Edinburgh. Eva's mother left Austria when Adolf Hitler came to power in Germany. She moved to Paris and then to London. While Eva's mother lived in London, writing film scripts, Eva lived with her father and a governess before beginning her education at the progressive Dartington School in Devon.

She went on to study science at university in London and Cambridge, but turned to teaching and writing after she was married in 1947, saying she preferred not to do experiments on animals. She began writing magazine stories and television dramas, publishing her first book for children, *The Great Ghost Rescue* in 1975. She became known for her witty, fantastical stories about wizards, witches,

harpies and ghosts, explaining that after her own unsettled childhood, she wanted to give children happiness through books.

After the death of her husband, Eva sought solace by writing more serious, historical novels, beginning with *Journey to the River Sea*. Set in the Amazon, and paying tribute to her husband's interest in ecology, it won the Smarties Gold Prize in 2001. She died at the age of 85 in October 2010, a few months before *One Dog and His Boy* was published.

Key facts

One Dog and His Boy

Author: Eva Ibbotson

Illustrator: Sharon Rentta

First published: 2011 by Scholastic Ltd

Awards: Shortlisted for the Galaxy National Book Awards, the Red House Children's Book Award and the Sheffield Children's Book Award.

Did you know: Eva Ibbotson's children's books have been shortlisted for many awards including the Carnegie Medal, the Guardian Children's Fiction Prize and the Roald Dahl Funny Prize. Her more serious fiction for older readers made her a bestselling author for adults in Germany.

Cover and blurb

Look together at the cover of the book. Ask: *What sort of story do you think this will be?* (Funny, a story about friendship, an adventure?) *What does the title imply?* (The dog 'owns' the boy rather than the other way around.) Read the dedication page. Next, read the back cover blurb. Ask what the children think the Easy Pets Dog Agency might be. What can they infer from the blurb? (That Hal's parents deceive him, as they have only rented a puppy for a weekend, but that Hal and the dog called Fleck will somehow fight to stay together.) What is the main 'hook' that makes the reader want to read the story? (To find out how Hal overcomes obstacles to keep Fleck.) Read the reviews on the cover (depending on the edition) picking out key descriptive words such as 'funny', 'observant', 'touching'.

Chapter 1

Discuss Hal's situation at home. (He lives in an opulent home with every comfort and toy a child could want, but all he wants is a dog.) Ask: *What idea does his father come up with, and why is it a trick?* (They will rent a dog, hoping that Hal will soon tire of it.) Ask the children to brainstorm descriptive words about the home ('plush', 'tidy', 'immaculate', 'luxurious'). Ask: *Why does Albina object to a dog?* (A dog might make a mess and spoil her lovely furnishings.)

Chapter 2

Ask: *How do the Carkers and their clients view the dogs?* (as accessories or belongings) Invite children's opinions on the Agency. Tell them that there genuinely are agencies that allow people to borrow dogs from owners. Ask: *How might they benefit owners and borrowers?* (They could help owners who cannot exercise their dogs enough; they allow people who cannot have a dog full-time to enjoy one on a temporary basis.) *How is this Agency different?* (The dogs have no permanent owners.) *How do the dogs feel about that?* (They long for a permanent, loving owner and home.) *What else do we learn about them?* (That they understand what humans say.) Refer to question 16 on the Guided Reading bookmark (page 12). Pause at the end of the chapter to ask why Kayley pretends the mongrel is a special 'breed'. (The Carkers and their clients are only interested in pedigree dogs.)

Chapters 3 and 4

At the end of Chapter 3, focus on question 9 on the Guided Reading bookmark. Ask: *What might happen if no one rents Fleck?* (He will be taken to the animal shelter and may be put down.) *What happens that suggests hope?* (Hal arrives to choose a dog.) Continue reading Chapter 4. Consider the chapter title and ask: *Is it really Hal who chooses?* (Fleck chooses him on first sight.) *How does this reinforce the book title?* (It is the dog that picks his owner.)

Chapters 5 and 6

Read on through Chapter 5, raising question 11 on the Guided Reading bookmark as the author describes Albina's friends, and using the character of Olga to prompt question 3 on the bookmark. Read Chapter 6 and discuss some of the ways Fleck has improved Hal's life (companionship, new friends, observing more, feeling safe in the dark). Refer to question 4 on the Guided Reading bookmark. Invite views on the trick his parents have played. Ask: *What do you think Hal might be going to do?* Suggest that Hal's reaction to his mother's revelation creates suspense as we wonder what he will do next.

Chapters 7 and 8

Read Chapter 7. Consider question 6 on the Guided Reading bookmark. Ask the children to summarise new characters or turns in the plot that they think might be significant (for example, Pippa, Hal's parents deciding they may send him to boarding school). Continue reading, discussing what kind of home Hal's grandparents have, and how it differs from his parents' home. Ask: *Do you think Hal would be happier living with his grandparents and, if so, why?*

Chapters 9 and 10

Read up to the reunion of Hal and Fleck in the restaurant. Consider question 2 on the Guided Reading bookmark. Read as far as the sentence 'Hal was tired of living in a grown-up world. It was time to make his own world…'. Ask: *How does the author build suspense here?* (We can tell that Hal is just going along with his parents' plans to keep them happy but really intends to take matters into his own hands.) *What do you think he might do?* Encourage them to speculate, taking care that children who may have read the story already do not spoil it for others.

Read on to the end of Chapter 10. Ask the children to explain what Hal had intended to do (break in and steal Fleck, then travel by train to his grandparents in Berwick). Ask: *Who or what has disrupted his plan?* (Pippa, by letting out the other dogs.) *Suggest another way that fate seems to have intervened in Hal and Fleck's story.* (Pippa was working at the Agency because Kayley was ill at home.)

Chapters 11 and 12

Ask the children how we can tell his grandparents understand Hal better than his parents. (They know he will not have forgotten the dog, and they suspect this is behind his disappearance.)

Discuss how Pippa tricks the circus owner into letting them stay. (She tells them Francine is part of an act trained by Elsa, a trainer he knows well.) Ask: *Are her fibs justified and if so why?* (It will help them and the dogs safely on their way to Berwick.) Consider question 14 on the Guided Reading bookmark.

Chapters 13 and 14

Discuss the superficial nature of Curzon's interests: money and appearances. Refer to question 13 on the Guided Reading bookmark. Ask: *How does this link in with a main theme?* Refer to question 15 on the bookmark and consider the character of Sprocket, a bumbling amateur sleuth. Ask: *What is the other chief source of humour in the story?* (The dogs' antics.) After Chapter 14, discuss question 10 on the Guided Reading bookmark. Ask*: In what way is Greystoke House similar to the Pets Agency?* (The children there are viewed rather like belongings or accessories by the prospective foster parents.) Focus on Francine. Ask: *Do you think she should have stayed?* Encourage them to give their reasons.

Chapters 15, 16 and 17

How are the dogs affecting or changing lives other than Hal's? (Li-Chee encourages Nini to talk again; Honey brings help and joy to Selby.) Ask: *What now threatens Hal and Pippa's plan?* (A circus lad has contacted the detective agency to claim the reward; the private investigator Sprocket is on their trail.) Discuss the hook this creates in the plot. (To find out if Hal and Pippa will be caught or will get to Berwick with the dogs.) What had just happened when the stable boy recognised Hal? (They had enjoyed the triumph of their dog act.) Pause to reflect how twists like this keep the plot lively.

Chapter 18

Read the first three paragraphs and check that the children understand the irony of 'Kevin Dawks was a kind man.' (His 'kindness' means getting rid of others' rubbish in exchange for money by illegally dumping it.) Pause at the point where Hal discovers the rubbish and consider question 12 on the Guided Reading bookmark. Read the rest of the chapter. Ask: *How has the threat to the children's plan now escalated?* (Kevin Dawks is after the reward too.)

Chapters 19 and 20

Ask: *What has distracted the tracker dogs in finding a trail?* (The blue flannel.) *Why is the monastery a fitting place for the runaways to find?* (St Roc is the patron saint of dogs.) Refer to question 7 on the Guided Reading bookmark. Explore together the pattern that has emerged in the story as Otto finds contentment at the monastery. (Pairings of dogs and people or places they love: Francine and the circus; Li-Chee and Nini; Selby and Honey.)

Chapter 21

Pause to identify the source of humour (poor Sprocket and his wild imaginings) and ask the children to explain the effect Otto has on the vicious tracker dogs. How does this fit in with the theme of the impact dogs can have in the story (question 3 on the Guided Reading bookmark)? (Dogs can change people, and now, we learn, they can change other dogs too.) Ask: *What do you feel as the children finally reach their destination? What do you think might happen now?*

Chapters 22, 23, 24 and 25

Raise question 8 on the Guided Reading bookmark. Challenge the children to summarise what happens. Review questions 5 and 13 on the Guided Reading bookmark. Consider the way the author tidies all the loose ends, and discuss whether they think it is a fairytale ending. (The two misfit characters, Sprocket and Queen Tilly are a perfect match for each other; the Fentons' former maid Olga gets a new job at Kayley's dog rescue, the home is called after the old family farm her grandfather yearns for and so on.) Do they think it is a good ending to the book? Ask them to give their reasons.

SCHOLASTIC
READ & RESPOND
Bringing the best books to life in the classroom

One Dog and His Boy
by Eva Ibbotson

Focus on...
Meaning

1. What would you say are the main themes in the story?

2. How do you think fate or destiny play a part in Hal's story?

3. In what ways do dogs change humans in the story?

4. What facts do we learn about dog behaviour in the novel?

Focus on...
Organisation

5. Identify three main storylines in the novel.

6. What are the significant turning points in the plot?

7. What pattern emerges in the story as the journey progresses?

8. What is the main hook that keeps us reading to the end?

SCHOLASTIC
READ & RESPOND
Bringing the best books to life in the classroom

One Dog and His Boy
by Eva Ibbotson

Focus on...
Language and features

9. How does the author create suspense?

10. When and how does the author speed up the pace?

11. How does the author use direct speech to convey character?

12. How does the author use rhetorical questions?

Focus on...
Purpose, viewpoints and effects

13. What moral issues does the author raise in the novel?

14. Would you have let the dogs free as Pippa did and, if so, why?

15. What are the main sources of humour in the novel?

16. In the story, the author describes the dogs' thoughts and feelings. Do you think this makes the story more effective?

Extract 1

- In this extract from Chapter 8, we first meet Hal's grandparents. Ask the children if they can recall where Hal's grandparents live. (On the Northumbrian coast.) Display the media resource 'Heading North map' to locate it, showing how far it is from London.

- Underline Alec's words 'Growing up in that museum – it's no life for a boy.' Discuss what he means: in what ways is Hal's home like a museum? (Everything is tidy and just for show or display and you are not allowed to make any mess.) Point out how Hal's grandparents' home is very different: Alec walks in with muddy boots and Marnie is doing something creative but messy – baking bread.

- Read aloud the final paragraph. Circle the words that describe the location: 'cottage', 'sand', 'golden curve', 'islands', 'rocky outcrop'. Underline the word 'distinct' and discuss what the sentence means. (It is a clear day so they can clearly see the offshore islands.) Ask: *What might it be like on other days?* (The islands might be shrouded in fog, sea mist or rain.)

- Highlight the boat's name, *Peggotty*, and explain that it is the name of a kind fisherman and his wife who bring up David, in the famous novel *David Copperfield* by Charles Dickens. Why is it appropriate? (Alec uses it as a fishing boat.)

- Ask the children what Hal might enjoy about living here with Fleck (playing on the beach, going out in the boat with his grandfather). Ask: *Would you prefer living in Hal's home or at the cottage?* Encourage them to give reasons.

Extract 2

- This extract is taken from Chapter 18, just before Kevin Dawks spots Hal by the roadside. Ask: *Why does Fleck run back to Hal?* (A piece of wire has got caught in his paw.) Discuss what Hal has discovered. (Rubbish dumped illegally in the countryside by Kevin Dawks.)

- What is the first thing that alerts Hal to the dump? (the smell) Highlight the sentence 'A vile sick-making stench of decay and rottenness.' Challenge the children to explain what is missing from the sentence grammatically (a verb) and ask them to suggest verbs to complete it (such as 'wafted over'/'rose up'/'hung in the air').

- Look together at the descriptive phrases that make the dumped rubbish sound disgusting ('vile sick-making…', 'heap of rotting food', 'stained upholstery', 'foetid bubbles of gas', 'this unspeakable smell'). Highlight them and discuss the image this creates. Focus on 'foetid' and ask the children if they can explain what would cause smelly bubbles of gas (bacteria or micro-organisms).

- Highlight these two phrases: 'half open tins of oil oozed' and 'braked, and backed towards him'. Say them aloud together, listening for the repetition of sounds. Remind the children that this is known as alliteration, and underline the repeated sounds.

- Discuss why the rubbish is damaging as well as unsightly. (It could harm animals as well as plants or trees like the young sapling.) Then briefly consider the moral that the author is raising here: how humans can ruin nature.

Extract 3

- This extract from Chapter 21 begins as Darth and Terminator pick up the scent of the runaways and start to chase them. Highlight the short sentence 'Then suddenly they understood.' Ask: *What do Hal and Pippa suddenly realise?* (That the vicious dogs are chasing them.) *Why is Otto missing?* (He has taken up his post and will stop them in their tracks). *What is ominous when the hounds stop barking?* (It shows that they are ready to attack and kill their prey.)

- Highlight the way the author creates a fast pace in this episode, considering vocabulary including strong active verbs ('leaped', 'streak', 'race', 'slither'), word order (such as the use of the fronted adverbial 'Terrified') and punctuation (such as the use of the exclamation mark and dash) and alliteration ('slither down the steep slope'; 'steep scramble').

- Point out the reference to Barry, the Swiss St Bernard dog famous for many rescues, who was stuffed and displayed in the Natural History Museum in Switzerland. Underline the words 'as if' and identify the simile. What does it suggest? (That Otto stands stock still and is also brave and proud.) Highlight the similes 'like creatures from the netherworld' and 'straight as arrows' and discuss their effects.

- Underline or circle tricky words ('netherworld', 'baying', 'fearsome', 'rending'). Discuss together what they mean, and suggest homonyms. Which other word in the text links to the netherworld? ('hellhounds')

- Circle language that describes the countryside where the chase takes place: 'low stone wall', 'steep slope', 'beach', 'gorse'. Point out how we know there are likely to be cows in the field: 'cowpats'.

- Ask: *What does the final sentence imply?* (That this is like a fox hunt, and the hounds will kill and tear apart their prey.)

Extract 4

- This is a non-fiction extract about Northumberland. Ask: *Who do you think the text is aimed at and where might it appear?* (A brochure or website to encourage people to visit the Northumbrian coast.)

- Revise persuasive writing, asking the children to pick out persuasive words and phrases ('Come to', 'enjoy', 'Take', 'Tuck into', 'You can', 'try'). Circle or underline them. Then highlight and discuss the words that make the area sound attractive ('beautiful', 'glorious', 'picturesque', 'stunning', 'spectacular', 'magnificent').

- Circle 'coasteering' and ask the children if they have heard of this adventure sport and can describe it. (Moving around a rocky coast by climbing, scrambling or swimming, without the use of any craft.) Circle or underline any other tricky words such as 'pelagic', again explaining the meaning (relating to the open sea).

- Highlight the simile 'sinuous grace like ballet dancers' and point out an example of alliteration 'stunning swathes of sandy bays'. Discuss how they make the extract more effective.

- Discuss the attractions of the coast (beaches, seaside attractions, wildlife, adventure sports). Which of these are described in the novel? (The golden sandy beaches, the offshore islands, the sea birds and seals, the rocky islets.) Highlight the fictional name of the offshore island in Extract 1 and suggest what it echoes here ('Farra' – 'Farne').

- Ask: *What do you think Hal would enjoy about living on the Northumbrian coast?* (Playing on the beach, playing at the penny arcades, eating fish and chips, rock pooling, going out in a fishing boat or cruise around the islands.) *What do you think Fleck would enjoy?* (The beaches, running and sniffing.)

Extract 1

Chapter 8

"There's a postcard from Hal," said Alec Fenton, coming into the cottage and stamping the mud off his boots. It was only a few steps to the shore where he kept his dinghy but it had rained in the night and the path easily turned to mud.

His wife, Marnie, who was kneading bread at the kitchen table, wiped her hands and smiled with pleasure. "Let's have a look, then."

It was a long time since they had been to London to visit Hal's parents, but they thought the world of their grandson.

Marnie read the card over her husband's shoulder.

"Well, that is good news! He's got a dog all for himself! I always said that was what Hal needed."

Alec nodded. "Growing up in that museum – it's no life for a boy."

He looked out of the cottage window. The tide was out, and the sand stretched in a golden curve to the water's edge. It was a quiet day and the islands were distinct: the big island, Farra, where the monks had lived in medieval times, the smaller low-lying island where their neighbour grazed his sheep, and the rocky outcrop where the seals came to breed. A cormorant dived from a rock and came up with a fish in his beak. The gulls circled. Alec's own boat, the *Peggotty*, was pulled up on the shore, ready for the evening's fishing.

Extract 2

Chapter 18

Fleck had been running ahead, but now he came back to Hal and stopped in front of him, holding up a front paw.

"What's the matter, Fleck?"

Fleck whimpered, and Hal saw a piece of rusty wire caught between his toes. Hal took it out, and it was then he noticed the smell.

It was a smell that seemed completely unreal in this lovely place. A vile sick-making stench of decay and rottenness.

Then he saw it: a pile of rubbish spilling down to the edge of the water. There was a torn mattress; half open tins of oil oozed on to the grass. A heap of rotting food burst out of a plastic bag, and an old sofa lay on its side, its rusty springs sticking up from the stained upholstery. Some of the refuse had been tipped into the stream itself; foetid bubbles of gas broke the surface of the water. A twisted electric fire was wedged against a boulder. A young birch sapling had fallen across the stream, broken by the weight of an iron bath.

And over everything, this unspeakable smell…

Hal hardly remembered how he got back up the bank. He was in a state of shock. Who could do this; who could turn this wonderful place into a hellhole? He was still getting his breath, tying up his shoelace at the edge of the road, when a pick-up drove past him, braked and backed towards him.

Extract 3

Chapter 21

Now they stopped at the place where Hal and Pippa had left the track, while the dogs sniffed the ground, trying to pick up a scent.

Then suddenly one of the figures shouted and pointed while the other bent down and slipped off the leashes. The next moment, two dark, squat shapes leaped the low stone wall, and howling like creatures from the netherworld, they began to streak off down the hill.

Even then the children could not at first believe what they were seeing – it seemed impossible. Then suddenly they understood. It wasn't hares or foxes that these hellhounds were chasing.

"It's us they're after," shouted Pippa. "They're hunting us!"

Terrified, they began to race and slither down the steep slope and all the time the baying became louder. There was no moment when they dared to look behind them, so they did not notice that Otto was no longer there.

He had stopped at the edge of the last steep scramble down to the beach and was standing as still as if he were Barry, his stuffed ancestor in the Natural History Museum, his silhouette outlined against the high blue of the early summer sky.

The two hellhounds ran straight as arrows towards him, ignoring gorse, cowpats, a clump of barbed wire. The muscles in their chests and forelegs were bunched, their upper lips curled back, showing even more of their fearsome teeth. Their eyes were red, saliva streaked down their necks and they had stopped barking. The shouting was over; the tearing and rending was about to begin.

Extract 4

Follow the North Sea Trail!

Come to the beautiful Northumbrian coastline and enjoy thirty miles of glorious beaches. Take a leisurely stroll along seafront piers, play at the penny arcades, and tuck into delicious freshly caught fish and chips. Explore picturesque fishing communities, dotted around stunning swathes of sandy bays. The coast path offers 5000 kilometres of coastal walking around the North Sea Basin.

On a clear day, you can see the Farne Islands, a cluster of almost thirty small islands and rocky outcrops lying a few miles off shore. Many of the islets are underwater at high tide. They are formed of whinstone, a rock prone to weathering and faulting vertically, which creates spectacular steps and sheer craggy rock faces above the water. These rocky outcrops are the most famous sea bird sanctuary in the British Isles and also home to a large colony of Atlantic Grey Seals.

You can explore the coast by taking a cruise around the islands. You can visit one of the bird sanctuaries or go seal spotting. An Atlantic Grey seal bull can weigh in at 300 kilograms and although clumsy and lumbering on land, they swim with sinuous grace like ballet dancers under the water. Take a fishing trip or a pelagic cruise to see larger mammals including dolphins, porpoises, minke or even killer whales.

If you enjoy adventure sports, you can go diving for wrecks, try the intrepid sport of coasteering, or go kite or wind surfing. Or if it's relaxation you are seeking, have a doze in a deck chair on one of the magnificent golden beaches while the children build sandcastles and go rock pooling.

GRAMMAR, PUNCTUATION & SPELLING

1. Which relative?

To use relative clauses. To use commas to clarify meaning.

Copies of *One Dog and His Boy*, photocopiable page 22 'Who, which, when?'

What to do

- Remind the children of the rental agency in the story, the Easy Pets Dog Agency. Ask volunteers to think up a factual statement about it, for example: 'The Easy Pets Dog Agency rented out dogs.'

- Using spoken language only, ask the children to say how the sentence could be extended using a relative pronoun such as 'who', 'which' or 'when'. For example: 'The Easy Pets Dog Agency, which was in a fashionable part of London, rented out dogs.'

- Again, without writing, challenge the children to use another relative pronoun to extend the sentence further: 'The Easy Pets Dog Agency, which was in a fashionable part of London, rented out dogs who did not have permanent owners.'

- Write the extended sentences on the board, with no punctuation, and ask the children where to insert commas to make the meaning clear. Underline the words within the commas and explain this is a relative clause.

- Hand out copies of photocopiable page 22 'Who, which, when?' for pairs to complete. Remind them to use punctuation to help divide up their long clauses.

Support: Provide the relative clauses for children to insert in the correct places (for example: 'who was standing in for her sister Kayley'.)
Extension: Ask pairs to write short statements about characters from the novel, and challenge each other to use relative pronouns to extend them.

2. Synonyms and antonyms

To find and use synonyms and antonyms.

Copies of *One Dog and His Boy*, interactive activity 'Pick a word', Extract 2.

What to do

- Remind the children what synonyms and antonyms are and then work through interactive activity 'Pick a word' together.

- When they are familiar with the exercise, re-read Extract 2 describing Hal's discovery of the rubbish dump. Ask the children to find the adjectives and write them on the board ('rusty', 'vile', 'sick-making', 'torn', 'rotting', 'foetid', 'twisted', 'unspeakable'). Using 'vile', suggest some synonyms (disgusting, horrible) and antonyms (lovely, gorgeous).

- Ask the children to work in pairs to find one or more synonyms and antonyms for each of the words on the board.

- As a class, work through their suggestions, making lists under each adjective of all the synonyms and antonyms they have found.

- Challenge them to work in their pairs to draft more descriptive words and phrases about the rubbish dump. They should write down phrases and then try to find synonyms and antonyms for as many of the adjectives as they can. Share their findings as a class.

Support: Work through the list of adjectives on the board together, writing a list of synonyms and antonyms as a shared activity.
Extension: Ask pairs to think of descriptive words or phrases that could be used to describe the countryside that Kevin Dawks is spoiling, and then write lists of synonyms and antonyms for the adjectives used.

3. Passive voice

Objective

To understand and use the passive voice.

What you need

Copies of *One Dog and His Boy*.

What to do

- Write two sentences on the board: 'Sprocket kept a cabinet full of disguises.'; 'A cabinet full of disguises was kept by Sprocket.' Underline the verbs, using the terms 'active verb' and 'passive verb'. Point out how the verb changes the sentence: the active verb puts the focus on Sprocket; the passive on the hoard of disguises.

- Expand each sentence: 'Sprocket kept a hoard of disguises. He liked being in disguise and stalking people.'; 'A cabinet full of disguises was kept by Sprocket. It contained moustaches, nose hair, pimples and boils.' Point to the object in each first sentence ('Sprocket' and 'A cabinet') and how it becomes the subject in each following sentence. Explain that passive verbs may be used to introduce someone or something that becomes the subject of the next sentence.

- Write 'The Easy Pets Dog Agency was owned by the Carkers.' Underline the passive verb 'was owned'. Ask the children to suggest the next sentence, for example: 'The Agency rented out dogs.'

- Together, brainstorm a list of characters or places in the novel. Challenge the children in pairs to write pairs of sentences about each subject, following the same pattern.

- Share sentences. Write the best examples on the board, underlining the passive verbs.

Differentiation

Support: Work through the sentences together to make children more familiar with the sentence pattern.
Extension: Challenge small groups to find other subjects from the novel and use them to make pairs of sentences including passive verbs.

4. Adverbials

Objective

To use adverbials.

What you need

Copies of *One Dog and His Boy*, photocopiable page 23 'Adding adverbials'.

What to do

- Begin by reminding the children that adverbs give information about verbs. Introduce the term 'adverbials' and explain that they are phrases that are used instead of adverbs. They can give us information about the time, place or manner in which something happens.

- Write on the board: 'Hal ran'. Add the words 'with a pounding heart' and explain that this is an adverbial which explains the manner in which he ran. Now add the words 'down the hill' to demonstrate an adverbial of place. Finally, add 'when he saw the vicious dogs' to demonstrate an adverbial of time.

- Now write three further sentences on the board: 'Kevin Dawks offered Hal a lift in his cab when he spotted him.'; 'Kevin Dawks spotted Hal beside the road.' and 'Kevin Dawks steered the cab sharply to the left.' Ask volunteers to identify and underline the adverbials, then say which type they are (time, place and manner).

- Hand out photocopiable page 23 'Adding adverbials' and ask pairs to complete them. Explain that the accuracy of the answer is not important – rather their use of the adverbials. When they have finished, share answers as a class.

Differentiation

Support: Provide a list of the answers and ask children to write them in the correct places on the photocopiable sheet.
Extension: Challenge children to work with a partner and each think up questions for their partner to answer using an adverbial.

5. List it

Objective

To use a colon to introduce a list and to use semicolons and bullet points within lists.

What you need

Copies of *One Dog and His Boy*, photocopiable page 24 'Make a list'.

Cross-curricular link

PSHE

What to do

- Ask pairs to scan Chapter 1 for the presents that Hal is given on his birthday. Bring the class back together, write on the board: 'Hal's birthday presents:' and point out the colon, explaining that a colon can be used to introduce a list. Ask the children for presents they spotted and write each item after a new bullet point, explaining what a bullet point is.

- Then show how to write a list using semicolons to separate each item and explain that semicolons tend to be used in a descriptive list, with longer items ('a giant, purple dinosaur with spotty legs; a great woolly mammoth, sitting under a tree; a long-nosed armadillo and two tiny centipedes'). Point out the 'and' that is used instead of a final semicolon.

- Ask children to scan Chapter 9 for things Albina thinks Hal will need for boarding school. In pairs, they should list the items, using a colon to introduce the list and either bullet points or semicolons for the items.

- Share the lists and check punctuation.

- Hand out photocopiable page 24 'Make a list' and ask pairs to complete it.

Differentiation

Support: Work through one of the lists on the photocopiable sheet together to establish familiarity with the punctuation.
Extension: Challenge children to compose more lists using material from the novel, punctuating them correctly.

6. Vowel spellings

Objective

To investigate spellings and learn some words specifically.

What you need

Extract 2, Copies of *One Dog and His Boy*, interactive activity 'Vowel search', dictionaries, thesauruses.

What to do

- Display Extract 2. Circle the word 'foetid' and focus on the spelling 'oe' (pronounced /f/ /e/ /t/ /i/ /d/ or /f/ /ee/ /t/ /i/ /d/). Say that the 'oe' spelling can also be pronounced /oa/ or /oo/, depending on the word. Explain that 'foetid' comes from a Latin root: the Latin word 'fetidus' (stinking) and verb 'fetere' (to stink) which may in English spellings have become blended with the Latin word 'fumus' (smoke). Tell the children that exploring word origins or 'roots' will help them to understand and learn tricky spellings.

- Display interactive activity 'Vowel search' and complete it in small groups. Review the spelling, pronunciation and meaning of each word. Provide groups with a dictionary and thesaurus and ask them to find the origins of each word. They should also draft a short sentence using each word, to bring out its meaning. Share their findings, writing the best sentences on the board.

- Encourage children to keep a record of new or tricky words that they find in the novel, and to use a dictionary or thesaurus to explore others with the same root and/or spelling pattern.

Differentiation

Support: The interactive activity could be a whole-class activity.
Extension: Provide words using the 'ae' spelling ('maelstrom', 'maestro', 'alumnae', 'paediatric') and tell children to repeat the exercise, finding word roots, pronunciation and meaning, and using them in sentences.

Who, which, when?

● Extend each sentence using the information in the box next to it. Use a relative pronoun ('who', 'which', 'when') and remember to add commas in the correct places. The first one has been done for you.

1. Greystoke House was on the outskirts of Todcaster.

   Greystoke House, which was a children's home, was on the outskirts of Todcaster.

   > Greystoke House was a children's home.

2. Pippa let out all the dogs in Room A.

   _____

   _____

   > Pippa was standing in for her sister Kayley.

3. Hal decided to run away from home.

   _____

   _____

   > His mother had returned Fleck to the Agency.

4. Hal bought two tickets to Berwick on Tweed.

   _____

   _____

   > Hal's grandparents lived in Berwick on Tweed.

5. Milton Sprocket was a private detective.

   _____

   _____

   > Milton's boss was Curzon Montgomery.

6. Barry was a famous St Bernard dog.

   _____

   _____

   > Barry stands in a museum in Bern, Switzerland.

7. Honey had been owned by a farmer.

   _____

   _____

   > Honey was a trained sheep dog.

Adding adverbials

● Answer the questions using different adverbials of time, place or manner. You can find the answers in the chapters shown, or create your answers from your memory of the story. The first one has been done for you.

1. How often were the dogs at the Easy Pets Dog Agency sprayed with perfume? (Chapter 2)

   The dogs were sprayed with perfume every day.

2. Where did Fleck go when he spotted Hal in the restaurant? (Chapter 9)

   _____

   _____

3. When did the clowns appear in the children's dog act? (Chapter 14)

   _____

   _____

4. How did Mrs Platt snore? (Chapter 15)

   _____

   _____

5. When did Milton Sprocket set off to find Hal? (Chapter 16)

   _____

   _____

6. Where was Hal when Kevin Dawks first spotted him? (Chapter 18)

   _____

   _____

7. When did Kayley discover the Carkers had vanished? (Chapter 25)

   _____

   _____

Make a list

- Choose two subjects below and make lists, finding the information in the book. Use a colon to introduce the list and either bullet points or semicolons for the items.

> - Objects in Hal's house
> - Names of the dogs in Room A at the Easy Pets Dog Agency
> - Skills of the dogs in Room A at the Easy Pets Dog Agency
> - Jobs that Kayley has to do every day at the Easy Pets Dog Agency
> - Disguises in Milton Sprocket's cabinet
> - Junk or rubbish that Kevin Dawks has illegally dumped

1. Hal's home

To draw inferences, justifying them with evidence.

Copies of *One Dog and His Boy*, interactive activity 'Albina's house rules'.

What to do

- Tell the children they are going to focus on Hal's home, describing what it is like and then drawing up a list of Albina's house rules.

- Begin by reading Chapter 1, then ask pairs to re-read it, skimming and scanning for any information they can find about the house (its location, rooms, furnishings, contents and so on).

- Share their findings, writing key facts on the board (for example: bathrooms, kitchen, Hal's bedroom, Albina's walk-in wardrobe, thick carpets, silk curtains and so on). Tell the children to draw a plan of the house as they imagine it and annotate or label it with all the information they have found.

- When they have finished, display interactive activity 'Albina's house rules'. Allow pairs time to skim and scan the text again for ideas for house rules (for example: 'No unpleasant smells allowed'; 'No flowers in the garden'). Encourage them to be creative and add their own ideas for rules that they think Albina might impose (for example, 'No eating crisps indoors'). Share ideas as a class.

Support: Skim and scan the text for evidence as a shared activity, writing information on the board to support children in drawing their plans and completing the house rules.
Extension: Encourage children to use their imagination to extend the house plans and rules with further ideas in keeping with the description in the text.

2. Canine characters

To describe characters.

Copies of *One Dog and His Boy*, photocopiable page 29 'A newcomer in Room A'.

PSHE

What to do

- As a class, come up with adjectives that describe character or personality ('kind', 'brave', 'cruel', 'sensible', 'lazy', 'deceitful', 'naïve', 'helpful', 'tactful', 'strong' and so on). Ask: *Which qualities do you think could also apply to a dog?*

- Divide the class into small groups, each with a note-taker. Each group chooses a dog from the story and decides on three adjectives to best describe it. They can use the list or think up their own. They should support each choice by citing evidence from the story ('Otto is strong and calm because he stands up to Darth and Terminator.'). Share the groups' ideas.

- Briefly review the devices the author uses to create the dog characters: physical description, habits, behaviour and actions.

- Challenge children to find examples of each device for their chosen dog character.

- Tell the children they are now going to invent a new dog that might join Room A. Hand out copies of photocopiable page 29 'A newcomer in Room A' for the children to complete.

- Invite volunteers to introduce their new dog, asking the class to judge which they think would make the most convincing new character and why.

Support: Children work in groups to invent a new dog.
Extension: Children write a short story featuring their new character.

3. Chance or Destiny?

Objectives

To draw inferences, justifying them with evidence. To ask questions to improve understanding.

What you need

Copies of *One Dog and His Boy*, photocopiable page 30 'Consequences'.

Cross-curricular link

RE

What to do

- Explain that this lesson will focus on the idea of destiny or fate guiding events in the novel, considering how destiny takes a part in Hal and Fleck's story, bringing them back together in spite of all the obstacles they face.

- Read Chapter 9 and together recount the chain of events that enable Hal and Fleck to be reunited. (The Gorlands hire Fleck and take him to the restaurant where Hal and his mother are having lunch.) Ask: *How likely do you think this would be to happen? Do you think it is just chance or has destiny taken a hand to bring the pair together?*

- Ask pairs to scan the novel for any other ways chance or destiny play a part in guiding events (for example, Kayley falls ill so Pippa is working at the Agency and lets out the dogs).

- Hand out photocopiable page 30 'Consequences' and ask pairs to complete it, using their own findings to help them.

- When they have finished, review the children's work, asking them to consider what other factors drive events in the plot (characters' decisions, the setting).

Differentiation

Support: Discuss the concept of fate, providing examples from the novel prior to group work.
Extension: Children draw a mind map showing how fate guides or alters events in the novel.

4. Narrative voice

Objective

To identify how language and structure contribute to meaning.

What you need

Copies of *One Dog and His Boy*.

What to do

- Tell the children they are going to focus on the narrative voice. Check that they understand the term 'narrator'. Ask: *Who narrates Hal's story?* (An all-seeing, all-knowing, anonymous narrator.) Ask them to suggest another narrator that the author could have used (for example Hal, writing in the first person, or Fleck). Invite children to suggest novels they have read with an animal narrator (for example, Michael Morpurgo's *War Horse*).

- Ask: *What are the advantages of the all-seeing narrator?* (The narrator knows what is going on at any time and with different characters, and is not limited to one viewpoint; they know how characters are feeling and why they act as they do.)

- Re-read Chapter 9 as far as 'who saw nothing but each other'. Tell the children they are going to try drafting the chapter in the first person, as either Hal or Fleck. Arrange the class into two groups, one to write as Hal, the other as Fleck.

- Allow the children time to draft a few paragraphs recounting the reunion as either Hal or Fleck.

- Invite volunteers to read their recounts. Discuss how changing the narrative voice affects the narrative. (Fleck will recall the Gorlands picking him out; Hal will recount the long, boring shopping trip before lunch with his mother.)

Differentiation

Support: Before they begin, scan the chapter together and make brief notes on the board for each character.
Extension: Children choose another episode to recount with Hal or Fleck as narrator.

5. Heading north

Objective

To describe settings.

What you need

Copies of *One Dog and His Boy*, media resource 'Heading north map', media resource 'Northumbria photographs'.

Cross-curricular link

Geography

What to do

- Ask the children to explain why Hal and Pippa travel north and where they are heading. (To Hal's grandparents on the Northumbrian coast.) Show media resource 'Heading North map' to remind children of Hal and Pippa's journey.

- Display media resource 'Northumbria photographs', and encourage them to describe how they imagine the place where Hal's grandparents live. Ask: *What are its key features?* (sea, cliffs, valleys, isolated cottages and farms and so on). Record their ideas.

- Ask pairs to scan the story for details about where Alec and Marnie live. Provide chapter references (Chapter 8 and Chapters 21 to 25) to help them. Prompt with questions such as: *What is the countryside like? What kind of animals or birds live there?* Children should record their findings.

- Bring the class back together and ask the children for more suggestions to add to the board.

- As a shared writing activity, compile a short description of this countryside, including the main features described in the text.

- Discuss the setting in the context of the book. Is it an important feature? (It provides a contrast with the wealthy but unhappy life Hal has at home.)

Differentiation

Support: Provide a detailed prompt list to help children find relevant information.
Extension: Encourage the children to find out more about the Northumbrian coastal habitat.

6. Storyboard

Objective

To summarise the main ideas drawn from more than one paragraph.

What you need

Copies of *One Dog and His Boy*, drawing materials.

Cross-curricular link

Art and design

What to do

- Read Chapter 18 together as far as 'while Pippa relocked the door'. Ask the children to summarise how Hal is abducted and how he escapes.

- Ask them to describe the location, skimming and scanning the text for details (a quiet country road leading up to the moors, the valley with the stream and bluebells, the stone hut and so on).

- Tell the children to imagine they are planning to film the scene for a movie. Explain that film-makers often make storyboards before filming – a sequence of pictures showing how the action develops.

- Put the children in pairs and let them re-read the chapter. Encourage them to decide which scenes they are going to illustrate for their storyboard.

- Ask the children to list six scenes and to write brief notes on what each scene should picture. Provide the prompts 'characters', 'setting', 'action'.

- Bring the class back together and write the best suggestions on the board. Discuss some of the detail that each scene could show (for example, Hal trapped in the stone hut, thumping on the door).

- Let the children, in their pairs, draw out the storyboards they have briefed.

Differentiation

Support: Scan the text together for possible scenes for the children to choose.
Extension: Let the children choose another episode to create a storyboard for in notes and pictures.

7. Plot drivers

Objectives

To summarise the main ideas drawn from more than one paragraph. To explain their understanding of what they have read, including through presentations.

What you need

Copies of *One Dog and His Boy*, interactive activity 'Problem? Resolution!', photocopiable page 31 'Plot drivers'.

Cross-curricular link

PSHE

What to do

- Read the closing paragraphs of the novel. Ask the children what they feel about the ending. Is it satisfactory? In what way is it similar to a fairy tale? Suggest that, like all fairy tales, the story contains problems that have to be resolved, before everything can end 'happily ever after'.

- Next, ask which characters face problems that have to be solved, encouraging the children to skim and scan the novel for information. Display interactive activity 'Problem? Resolution!' and record the children's answers in the 'problem' column. Encourage them to be concise.

- Ask pairs to refer to the story and make notes on how each problem is resolved before discussing as a class and completing the interactive activity.

- Hand out photocopiable page 31 'Plot drivers' for children to complete. They then cut out the boxes and paste them in the correct order, following the plot of the story.

- Ask children to present and explain their answers to the class.

Differentiation

Support: Remind the children of key facts or events to help them with their analysis.
Extension: Children can arrange the boxes from the photocopiable sheet as flow charts showing the connection between problem and resolution.

8. Creating suspense

Objectives

To identify how structure contributes to meaning. To discuss how authors use language, considering the impact on the reader.

What you need

Copies of *One Dog and His Boy*, printable page 'Suspense'.

Cross-curricular link

History

What to do

- Look at the chapter titles. Ask the children to suggest questions they raise, and how they create interest or suspense. For example: *Who or what has caused sorrow?* (Chapter 7); *Which dog needs to be rescued?* (Chapter 9); *Where has Hal gone?* (Chapter 11).

- Tell the children they are going to examine ways the author creates suspense, making us want to read on to find out what happens. Demonstrate this by reading the last two sentences of Chapter 13, 'Sprocket smiled and rubbed his hands. He was just in the mood for an important and tricky case.' Invite the children to consider how this hooks the reader, making the reader wonder what Sprocket will do. Discuss how the words 'smiled' and 'rubbed his hands' give the impression that Sprocket will really enjoy chasing the boy.

- Ask children to work in pairs. Hand out printable page 'Suspense' and ask pairs to look up each quote in the book and discuss together how it creates suspense at that point in the story. Allow them time to make notes, then share findings as a class.

Differentiation

Support: Provide page references to help children find key text.
Extension: Ask pairs to skim and scan the novel looking for any other sentences or parts of the text that create suspense. Suggest they focus on key turning points in the plot.

A newcomer in Room A

- Invent a new dog for Room A at the Easy Pets Dog Agency.

Name _____   Breed _____

Appearance _____
_____

Personality _____
_____
_____
_____
_____

Background/history _____
_____
_____
_____

- Draw the new dog here.

Consequences

● How do these chance events affect the plot? Explain their consequences.

Event	Consequence
Kayley is ill	
Albina takes Hal out to lunch at the restaurant where the Gorlands are eating	
Petroc has to go to hospital	
Mick sits next to Hal at the Circus	
The stable boy at the Circus spots the runaways	
Kevin Dawks sees Hal by the roadside	

Plot drivers

- Explain how each of the following items is significant in the plot.
- Then cut out and paste the boxes in the order in which they feature in the story.

✂

A letter
A rubbish heap
A restaurant
A circus
A monastery
A stone hut

TALK ABOUT IT

1. All I want

To use spoken language to develop understanding through speculating, hypothesising, imagining and exploring ideas. To précis longer passages.

What you need

Copies of *One Dog and His Boy*, photocopiable page 35 'My best friend'.

Cross-curricular link

PSHE

What to do

- Read Chapter 5 from 'That night, lying on the floor…' to '…now he had a protector and a friend.' Ask the children to summarise how Hal feels about having a dog (that it is much better than he ever imagined). Encourage them to précis some of the unexpected joys and list them on the board. Ask them if they can think of anything they felt that way about – it might be a pet, an experience, a holiday, a party. Invite children to voice their memories and encourage feedback and comparisons.

- Ask: *Can you think of a time when you had looked forward to something that ended up being a disappointment – like Hal's holiday in the Seychelles?* Again, encourage volunteers to raise their own experiences, and give reasons.

- Hand out photocopiable page 35 'My best friend' and tell the children to fill it in as if they are Hal writing about Fleck, and to use evidence from Chapter 5 of the novel.

Differentiation

Support: Review the photocopiable sheet and skim and scan the novel for evidence as a shared activity, before children fill it in.
Extension: Encourage children to use the photocopiable sheet as a model to record their own personal experience of a pet, or someone that they love.

2. Dog rules

Objective

To articulate and justify opinions. To participate in discussions. To explain and discuss their understanding of what they have read.

What you need

Copies of *One Dog and His Boy*, photocopiable page 36 'Hal and Fleck'.

Cross-curricular link

PSHE

What to do

- Tell the children they are going to think about how, in the novel, the author treats the idea of owning a dog and the benefits and responsibilities it brings. Remind the children of the inversion in the title: it is Fleck who 'owns' Hal, not the other way around.

- Write the heading 'Owning a dog' on the board, and underneath write two subheadings: 'Benefits' and 'Responsibilities'.

- Allow children time to discuss in small groups, appointing a note-taker to jot down ideas under each heading. If any children have dogs at home, encourage them to think how they enhance their lives, but also the commitment and time they require.

- Share notes as a class, recording children's ideas. Work through each one, encouraging children to cite evidence from the novel, as well as their own experience, in support. Benefits could include making new friends (Hal meets Pippa and also the blonde girl in the park). Responsibilities include: protecting from dangers (rusty wire/splintery bones).

- Hand out photocopiable page 36 'Hal and Fleck' and ask pairs to complete it.

Differentiation

Support: Provide groups with questions to help prompt ideas (such as: *What does a dog owner need to do every day?*).
Extension: Challenge groups to research how dogs can improve our health and well-being.

3. Viewpoints

Objectives

To participate in discussions, presentations and role play. To draw inferences, such as inferring characters' feelings, thoughts and motives.

What you need

Copies of *One Dog and His Boy*.

Cross-curricular links

PSHE, drama

What to do

- Read Chapter 9 from '"It's absolutely extraordinary," said Albina…' to '…right and fair and as they ought to be.'

- Discuss how Hal is feeling (Angry? Disappointed? Resentful?). Write suggestions on the board. Ask: *Would you feel as Hal does?* Encourage children to give their opinions.

- Ask: *Why does Hal seem 'calm and quiet'?* (He now knows what he has to do.) *Why doesn't he tell his father how he is really feeling?* (He no longer trusts his parents or believes he can persuade them.)

- Arrange the class into three groups. Assign one Hal, another Donald Fenton and the third Albina. Each group should discuss and take notes explaining their character's viewpoint at this stage in the story. For example, Albina might say 'I like to keep a smart house. I hate the idea of a messy dog spoiling it.'

- Ask a volunteer from each group to deliver a short speech presenting their character's viewpoint.

- Check they understand the term 'mediation'. Ask volunteers to suggest what a mediator might say to reconcile the parties. How could his parents rebuild Hal's trust?

Differentiation

Support: Work through character notes as a class activity before asking groups to draft short speeches in character.
Extension: Ask children to plan and perform a short role play of a family mediation session.

4. Working dogs

Objectives

To articulate and justify opinions. To participate in discussions and debates.

What you need

Copies of *One Dog and His Boy*, interactive activity 'Animal issues'.

Cross-curricular links

PSHE, history

What to do

- Ask the children to suggest different types of working dog mentioned or featured in the novel, recording their suggestions (sheep dog, guide dog, guard dog, rescue dog). They should cite relevant names and evidence from the book. Encourage them to add their own ideas to the list (for example: hearing dog, assistance dog, sniffer dog).

- Discuss the skills or abilities that different 'work' requires (scenting, loyalty, bravery, good vision).

- Ask: *Do you think dogs enjoy working? If so, why?* (Dogs, by nature, enjoy pleasing their owner or trainer; some are bred to have herding or hunting instincts.) *Is there any 'work' you would object to dogs doing?* (Fox hunting? Using dogs in war? Dangerous jobs, such as sniffing out explosives?)

- Organise a class debate with the subject 'Should dogs be made to work for people?', exploring the arguments for and against. Appoint debate leaders to give views on either side and encourage others to support or oppose their arguments, giving reasons.

- Extend this activity into an exploration of how humans treat animals, using activity 5, 'Animal issues'.

Differentiation

Support: List key arguments under headings 'for' and 'against' on the board, before the debate.
Extension: Set the children the task of finding out more about dogs that have won bravery awards and also dogs that work in wars, to inform the debate.

5. Animal issues

Objectives

To explain and discuss their understanding of what they have read. To provide reasoned justifications for their views; to participate in debates.

What you need

Copies of *One Dog and His Boy*, interactive activity 'Animal issues', media resource 'Dog images'.

Cross-curricular link

PSHE

What to do

- Begin by re-reading Chapter 12 together. Focus on the two paragraphs beginning '"Why is it a Circus for Today?"' and Pippa's explanation that only the animals that are 'tame already' are used in the circus. What were circuses like before and why were the rules changed?

- Ask: *Does the novel present a positive or negative view of dogs performing in circuses?* Discuss children's opinions. Display interactive activity 'Animal issues' and encourage the children to find and discuss evidence from the text, noting their ideas. Display media resource 'Dog images' to stimulate ideas. For example, Francine enjoys performing with Rupert, which is a positive view of dogs performing in circuses. Albina initially gets excited in the Pampered Pooch shop by all the glamorous accessories (Chapter 25). Ask: *What does it show us about Albina? What would Hal think about the shop?*

- When they have finished, broaden the discussion on one or more issues, inviting views for and against, and encouraging a range of opinions.

Differentiation

Support: Before attempting the interactive activity, review the issues together, discussing how they feature in the novel.

Extension: Ask children to hold a debate on whether animals should be used in circuses.

6. Messages

Objectives

To explain and discuss their understanding of what they have read. To provide reasoned justifications for their views.

What you need

Copies of *One Dog and His Boy*, photocopiable page 37 'Changes'.

Cross-curricular link

PSHE

What to do

- Tell the children to consider the ending of the story and ask: *What lessons do you think Hal's parents have learned?* Encourage children to give opinions, along with evidence from the novel. Ask: *What evidence is there that Donald has changed and what has changed him?* (Realising what is really important when Hal went missing; visiting his old childhood home.) *What evidence is there that Albina has changed?* (She wants to buy material things for Fleck just as she did for Hal but resists and lets Hal choose.) *How might Hal's life change now?*

- Ask small groups to discuss what they think are the author's main 'messages' in the story. Allow them time, and suggest they appoint a note-taker to jot down key ideas.

- Bring the class back together and invite volunteers from each group to précis the author's main 'messages'. (That material things should not be valued as much as love, courage, friendship and enjoyment of the simple things in life, like going to the park or enjoying nature.) Compare responses, encouraging children to provide evidence.

- Hand out photocopiable page 37 'Changes' for children to complete before sharing findings.

Differentiation

Support: Provide chapter or page numbers to help children find relevant information.

Extension: Encourage children to identify and discuss other key themes in the novel.

My best friend

● Imagine you are Hal and write notes about how Fleck has changed your life. Use evidence from Chapter 5 of the story.

How he helps me see more.

_____

_____

_____

Why he helps me think more.

_____

_____

_____

Why he makes me laugh.

_____

_____

_____

How he stops me being afraid.

_____

_____

_____

How he is my best friend.

_____

_____

_____

Hal and Fleck

● List four things that Hal does for Fleck.

1.	2.

3.	4.

● List four things that Fleck does for Hal.

1.	2.

3.	4.

Changes

- Complete the chart to show how and why each character changes in *One Dog and His Boy*.

	How does each character change?	What changes them?	How do they remain the same?
Hal			
Fleck			
Donald Fenton			
Albina Fenton			
Milton Sprocket			

GET WRITING

1. Milton's poetry

To describe settings, characters and atmosphere.

Copies of *One Dog and His Boy*, photocopiable page 41 'Milton Sprocket'.

What to do

- Tell the children they are going to focus on the character of Milton Sprocket. Ask them to summarise how they see him, encouraging them to use a range of descriptive vocabulary.

- Write on the board the headings 'Appearance', 'Behaviour' and 'Actions'.

- Ask pairs to skim and scan the novel, looking for details about Sprocket to go under each heading. Pairs could concentrate on one heading, scanning one or more chapters from the following: 13, 16, 19, 21 and 25. Ensure that all chapters are covered by the class.

- When they have finished, bring the class back together and review their findings, writing key words or phrases on the board.

- Ask: *What does the character of Sprocket contribute to the book?* (Humour, pathos. Explain that 'pathos' means the reader sometimes feels sorry for Sprocket.) Referring to the list of character traits, examine which are a source of humour, for example his awful disguises ('Somewhere on the way he had lost his deeply loved moustache') or his terrible poems (Chapters 13 and 25).

- Hand out photocopiable page 41 'Milton Sprocket' and ask the children to complete it, working in pairs.

Support: Provide pairs of rhyming words to help children write their rhymes (for example: 'meat'/'neat'; 'brush'/'rush'; 'flower'/'power'; 'fish'/'swish').
Extension: Challenge the children to write a job application that Milton Sprocket might compose applying for a top detective job.

2. Easy Pets dogs

To identify audience and select appropriate form for purpose of writing.

Copies of *One Dog and His Boy*, interactive activity 'Dog classes'.

Science

What to do

- Display interactive activity 'Dog classes' and challenge the children to match the correct names to the photographs.

- Arrange children in pairs and ask them to suggest different ways the dogs available for hire in the Easy Pets Dog Agency could be classified: for example, by the type of work they do (sheep or rescue dog), by their breed, by their size/age/nature. Allow them time to discuss their ideas, then share suggestions on the board. Which would be most useful for prospective temporary or permanent owners? Encourage them to give reasons.

- Tell them they are going to draft advertisements for some of the dogs, including key information on their breed, skills, size, age, nature and so on. The adverts should be concise but should also contain information that a prospective owner would require.

- When they have finished, invite volunteers from pairs to read aloud their advertisements and encourage feedback. Have they missed out any key information? Which would be most useful to someone thinking of hiring a dog from the agency and why?

Support: Model one of the advertisements on the board as a shared activity before pairs begin work.
Extension: Tell children to choose one dog or role from the interactive activity to draft a first-person recount about its work and experiences.

3. Hal's alibi

Objectives

To participate in role play and improvisations. To perform their own compositions.

What you need

Copies of *One Dog and His Boy.*

What to do

- Ask the children if they can recall the alibi (checking they understand the term) that Hal uses when he runs away. (His parents think he is going to spend a night at his old school friend, Joel – Chapter 9.)

- Tell them they are going to plan and rehearse a scene in which Hal persuades Joel to give him an alibi.

- Arrange the class in pairs. Tell them to discuss and make notes for their scene. Ask: *What might Hal say to persuade his friend? What would he need to explain about what had been going on? How might Joel respond? Might he try to persuade Hal against his plan, and if so why?* Extract key ideas for them to develop. (Hal: parents have tricked me; Fleck needs me; my grandparents will understand. Joel: it's too dangerous; my parents might find out; we would both get in trouble.)

- Allow them time to make notes then tell them to rehearse a scene in which Hal persuades Joel to give him his alibi. Observe pairs as they practise and invite some to perform their scenes for the class.

Differentiation

Support: Work through the ideas on the board arranging them into arguments and counterarguments, to help children structure their dialogue before they begin.

Extension: Briefly revise the layout of a play script (dialogue and stage directions) then let pairs draft their scenes as play scripts.

4. Famous dogs

Objectives

To retrieve, record and present information from non-fiction. To plan their writing by selecting the appropriate form.

What you need

Copies of *One Dog and His Boy*, photocopiable page 42 'Historic hounds', internet access.

Cross-curricular link

History

What to do

- Ask the children if they can recall two famous dogs mentioned in the novel (Greyfriars Bobby, chapter 7, and Barry, a famous mountain rescue dog, chapters 12 and 21). What facts about either can they learn from the novel? Write their findings on the board.

- Explain they are going to find out some more about these famous dogs. They will then write a short biography about each for a book about famous dogs. Hand out photocopiable page 42 'Historic hounds' and read about Rin Tin Tin. Discuss the way the biography is written and the key facts included. (His name, story from birth to death, key dates, where he was from, what made him famous.)

- Provide access to the internet. Tell small groups to find out as much as they can about the famous dogs and appoint a note-taker to take down notes. They should then work individually to fill in the photocopiable sheet using the material they have found. Remind them to use the style of a biography.

- Bring the class back together and invite volunteers to read their entries aloud, encouraging feedback. Which are most effective, concise and informative?

Differentiation

Support: Provide a prompt list of questions to guide children in their research.

Extension: Challenge groups to research more famous dogs to extend the photocopiable sheet.

GET WRITING

5. A postcard from Hal

Objectives

To draw inferences, such as inferring characters' thoughts, feelings and motives. To select appropriate form for purpose of writing.

What you need

Copies of *One Dog and His Boy*, examples of informal letters and postcards (either real or from the internet).

What to do

- Read Chapter 8. Tell the children they are going to write the postcard that Hal sends to his grandparents, and also the letter that they send in reply. Refer to examples of postcards and informal letters, briefly considering style, layout and presentation.

- Ask pairs to scan the story for ideas to include, with one focusing on the postcard and the other on the letter. They can make notes from the novel then use their imaginations to add content. Provide examples to get them started. (Hal writes in his postcard that he has got a dog, Fleck. He might also tell them that Fleck makes him laugh, and they have fun together in the park. Alec and Marnie tell Hal that they would love him to visit and bring Fleck. They might also add that their Labrador, Meg, would love having a new playmate to stay.)

- Allow them time to make notes before drafting their postcards and letters. Encourage partners to review each other's work with constructive feedback.

- Bring the class back together and invite volunteers to read their cards and letters aloud.

Differentiation

Support: Skim and scan early chapters together for ideas for content.
Extension: Set pairs the challenge of writing the letter Hal and Pippa leave for Bill and Myra at the circus.

6. A dog for Dawks

Objectives

To plan their writing by noting and developing initial ideas. To describe characters in narratives.

What you need

Copies of *One Dog and His Boy*, photocopiable page 43 'A dog for Dawks'.

Cross-curricular link

PSHE

What to do

- Remind the children how dogs enhance and change lives in the novel – not just Hal's life but also that of other characters such as Nini, Old Selby and Sprocket. Ask: *Do you think a dog might be good for Kevin Dawks?* Encourage them to give their opinions and discuss whether he could be trusted with a dog or whether he might use a dog for crime or to frighten people.

- Tell them they are going to invent a dog that might change or reform Kevin Dawks for the better. Hand out photocopiable page 43 'A dog for Dawks' for pairs to complete, encouraging them to discuss their ideas together.

- When they have completed their notes, ask children to work alone to draft a few paragraphs describing how Dawks first meets his new canine companion then invite volunteers to read their work aloud, encouraging constructive feedback.

Differentiation

Support: Before children begin work on the photocopiable sheet, discuss some of the ways a dog might change Dawks (helping him enjoy countryside walks; teaching him to care about someone other than himself and so on).
Extension: Ask children to draft a short story about Dawks and his dog, which shows how it the dog has changed him.

Milton's Poems

- Choose two of these vans from the box below and create a short rhyme that Milton Sprocket might use for each one.

> ★ A butcher's van ★ A fishmonger's van
> ★ A painter and decorator's van ★ A florist's van

Historic Hounds

● Read this information about a dog named Rin Tin Tin.

Rin Tin Tin was a German Shepherd dog who had been rescued as a puppy from a World War 1 battlefield, by an American serviceman, Lee Duncan. Duncan took him home to California, and trained him to work in silent films. The dog appeared in 27 Hollywood movies, and became so famous for his expressive face and clever tricks, that in 1932, regular radio programmes were interrupted to announce his death.

● Use the internet to find out about these famous dogs. Write notes next to their picture.

Greyfriars Bobby

_____

_____

_____

_____

Barry the St Bernard of Bern

_____

_____

_____

_____

A dog for Dawks

● Imagine a dog that would help Kevin Dawks become a good man. Write your ideas below.

Name:_____   Breed:_____

Appearance and character:_____

_____

Its background/history:_____

_____

_____

Notes on how the dog changes Dawks:_____

_____

_____

A picture of the dog:

ASSESSMENT

1. Three words

Objectives

To describe characters. To maintain attention, staying on topic and initiating and responding to comments.

What you need

Copies of *One Dog and His Boy*, flash cards with the names of 'Pippa', 'Albina', 'Kevin Dawks', 'Milton Sprocket'.

Cross-curricular link

PSHE

What to do

- Write 'Hal' on the board and challenge the children to think of three adjectives that best describe his character. Emphasise that they need to be able to back up their suggestions with evidence from the novel (for example: 'brave' – he ventures on his journey alone with Fleck; 'clever' – he tricks his parents into believing him; 'persuasive' – he persuades his parents to let him keep Fleck).

- List the best adjectives on the board. Encourage children to evaluate each suggestion. (Is he brave, or is he actually foolhardy? Are there other events or actions in the novel that would support one or other judgement?)

- Arrange the class in small groups. Display the character flash cards, one at a time, allowing them time to discuss and list three adjectives that best describe each character, along with evidence. Encourage them to listen to each other's suggestions and to ask questions to ensure they agree on their choices.

- Bring the class back together and ask groups to share their adjectives, writing the best suggestions on the board and reviewing differences in choice.

Differentiation

Support: Help children come up with adjectives by compiling a list of actions for each character.
Extension: Add to the flash cards other topics such as plot and setting to extend the activity.

2. Themes

Objectives

To identify and discuss themes. To participate in discussions and presentations.

What you need

Copies of *One Dog and His Boy*, photocopiable page 47 'Novel themes'.

Cross-curricular link

RE

What to do

- Begin by asking the children if they can identify the main themes of the novel. Ask them to support their suggestions with reasons: for example, 'I think the bond between people and dogs is the main theme because dogs make everything better in the story'; or 'I think the main theme is not to give up on your dreams, because Hal makes his dream happen'.

- Write their suggestions for themes on the board and discuss which, if any, they would identify as the most important theme, again encouraging them to give reasons.

- Hand out photocopiable page 47 'Novel themes' and tell the children to discuss each theme, working in pairs. They then complete the sheet individually, writing their answers as full sentences (for example: 'Always follow your dreams – Hal finds happiness because he never gives up on his dream of owning a dog.').

- Bring the class back together and ask volunteers to present their choice of the most important theme.

Differentiation

Support: Let the children focus on two or three themes from the photocopiable sheet, working as a group.
Extension: Invite pairs to consider the themes listed on the photocopiable sheet, and suggest and discuss other novels they have read which echo them.

3. Spelling bee

Objective

To investigate spelling and understand that the meaning of some words needs to be learned specifically.

What you need

Copies of *One Dog and His Boy*.

What to do

- Explain that the class is going to hold a spelling bee based on words in the novel. Write word categories on the board such as character descriptions, setting-related words, topics (dogs, travelling circus, private detectives) or word types such as verbs, adverbs, adjectives.

- Arrange the class in groups of up to six. Allocate each group one category for the spelling bee. Explain that they need to search the novel for words for a spelling test. They should try to find challenging words in that category. For example, words based on setting could include: 'monastery', 'industrial', 'moorland.' Remind them to copy the spelling accurately.

- Allow each group time to compile eight words for the spelling bee.

- The groups can compete against each other in the spelling bee. They take turns to read out words from their lists (nominating a different speaker each time). The other group should confer and write down the correct spelling.

- Award points for the group with the most correct spellings and invite suggestions about which words were the hardest to spell.

Differentiation

Support: Help groups select chapters or parts of the novel that will be most productive for their word search.

Extension: Challenge groups to use a thesaurus to find other words with the same or a similar meaning to replace the words on their list for the spelling bee.

4. Which genre?

Objectives

To ask questions to improve understanding.
To identify and discuss themes and conventions.

What you need

Copies of *One Dog and His Boy*.

What to do

- Ask the children to nominate their favourite parts of the story. Ask: *Which parts do you find most exciting? Which are sad or funny?* Encourage them to give reasons.

- Ask: *What genre do you think the story fits into?* Suggest that it might combine elements of several genres (for example, it is both an adventure and a humorous story).

- Discuss key ingredients that make it an adventure (characters who have to go on a long journey and face risks and dangers; a fast-moving plot with surprises and cliff-hangers – events that make the reader want to read on to find out what happens next). Write suggestions on the board.

- Focus on humour and discuss key ingredients (for example, the hapless character of Milton Sprocket; the slapstick scene when Fleck is reunited with Hal in the restaurant). Again, list ideas on the board.

- Challenge the children to work in pairs to write a brief back cover blurb for the novel, bringing out the key elements of adventure and/or humour. When they have finished, bring the class back together and invite volunteers to read their blurb aloud, inviting feedback and criticism. Write the best blurbs on the board.

Differentiation

Support: Provide examples of effective back cover blurbs from this and other novels in similar genres.

Extension: Encourage pairs to design the back cover for a new edition, using their blurb and drafting short quotations from reviews.

5. Talking books

Objective

To give well-structured explanations, including expressing feelings. To articulate and justify answers, arguments and opinions.

What you need

Copies of *One Dog and His Boy*.

What to do

- Explain that the children are going to imagine they are appearing on the radio for a book club programme, reviewing the novel *One Dog and His Boy*.

- Discuss some questions that the programme's presenter might ask, and list them on the board. For example:
  - *Did you enjoy the novel and if so, why?*
  - *What is your favourite part of the novel and why?*
  - *Which character did you like best?*
  - *Did you feel the ending was satisfactory?*

- Allow the children time to work on their own to prepare some notes on what they think or feel about the novel. Encourage them to refer to the novel and to support their views with evidence. For example: 'I like the way Hal overcomes his problems because he refuses to give up on his dream.'

- Appoint a presenter who will give a brief introduction to the book, and then invite others to participate in a group discussion about the novel. The presenter can use the questions on the board and add more of their own.

Differentiation

Support: Children could work in pairs to discuss their opinions of the novel before they begin the book club discussion.

Extension: Encourage the children to use computing skills to make a podcast or video of the book club discussion.

6. Canine quiz

Objective

To articulate and justify answers, arguments and opinions. To participate in discussions and presentations.

What you need

Copies of *One Dog and His Boy*, interactive activity 'Canine quiz'.

What to do

- Tell the children they are going to try answering a multiple choice quiz about the novel.

- Open interactive activity 'Canine quiz' and let small groups attempt to answer the questions. They can check their scores when they finish, and compare scores between groups.

- When they have completed this task, challenge groups to compile their own quiz questions about the novel. They could attempt another multiple choice quiz, or write statements for a 'true or false' quiz. Encourage them to refer to the text to check that their answers are correct before they test another group. Model some examples on the board: 'Otto once worked as a mountain rescue dog.' True or false? (F); 'Darth and Terminator pick up the scent of Fleck's flannel.' True or false? (T)

- Groups can then challenge each other to answer their quiz questions. When they have finished, review scores and announce winning teams or groups.

- Encourage feedback, identifying which quiz questions were most challenging and why.

Differentiation

Support: Model further questions for each type of quiz on the board before groups begin, and brainstorm some quiz questions or statements together.

Extension: Invite groups to attempt to devise more difficult or challenging quizzes about the novel.

Novel themes

● Explain how these themes feature in the novel.

Dogs change people for the better

_____

_____

_____

Material possessions don't bring happiness

_____

_____

_____

Always follow your dreams

_____

_____

_____

A Journey

_____

_____

Trust and deceit

_____

_____

_____

_____

Friendship

_____

_____

SCHOLASTIC

Available in this series:

978-1407-14220-3

978-1407-14219-7

978-1407-14224-1

978-1407-14222-7

978-1407-14223-4

978-1407-15875-4

978-1407-14225-8

978-1407-15877-8

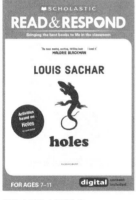

978-1407-14228-9

978-1407-14231-9

978-1407-14226-5

978-1407-14227-2

978-1407-14230-2

978-1407-15876-1

978-1407-15879-2

978-1407-14229-6

To find out more, call: 0845 6039091

or visit our website www.scholastic.co.uk/readandrespond